Unveiling the Veil: Black Women's Struggle for Political Equity

JENNIFER D. MOORE

Dedication

This book is dedicated to the resilient and courageous Black women who have navigated the challenges of political life, overcoming cultural discrimination and oppression. Your commitment to justice, equality, and accountability is a true inspiration that strengthens our resolve.

Intro
'Unveiling the Veil: Black Women's Struggle for Political Equity'
delves into the history and present political odyssey of Black women
as they strive for political equity in the past, present, and future. The
book examines how race, gender, and class intersect to shape Black
women's political experiences and their often overlooked but crucial
role in social and political movements. This book highlights the
challenges and barriers that Black women face in achieving political
equity, while also providing evidence of their political achievements
and resilience. It argues in support of greater recognition and support
for Black women's ongoing struggle for justice and representation
within a historical context. Understanding the political activism of
Black women is essential for various reasons. Their organizing is
shaped by intersecting and conflicting oppressions that intersect and
clash simultaneously. Their political activism helps to reveal how
and where these forces converge and diverge. Black women have
played significant roles in key historical moments such as slavery,
abolitionism, civil rights, feminism, and more. Studying their
organizing efforts sheds light on these pivotal moments.

Black women are still not adequately represented in national and state political leadership, despite their significant contributions. Their activism serves as a demonstration of the challenges they encounter in the political sphere and the importance of acknowledging diverse leadership in policy making and governance. Through their political activism, Black women redefine the concept of identity and move beyond single-issue politics. This highlights the broader struggles for equality and justice and provides a deeper understanding of the significance of their activism.

By expressing their viewpoints and input, they emphasize the necessity for a revitalized political conversation grounded in intersectionality and inclusiveness. Numerous concerns at the forefront of black women's advocacy, such as racial justice, reproductive rights, economic fairness, and healthcare accessibility, significantly affect the development and enforcement of policies. Examining black women's political mobilization can also provide insights into how activists present and support these concerns. Inclusivity. Many issues central to black women's activism, including racial justice, reproductive rights, economic equity, and healthcare

Chapter 1 Historical Context

Black women's involvement in political activism has a long-standing historical foundation, as they have actively participated in the fight against racism and various forms of oppression. From the era of slavery to the present day, black women have played a crucial role in advocating for civil rights, women's rights, and social justice. Below is a summary of some key figures and events within this rich legacy.

The Abolition Movement in the 19th century saw active participation from African American women throughout the country, advocating for the end of slavery. Sojourner Truth was a prominent voice speaking out on behalf of all slaves, and Harriet Tubman's Underground Railroad facilitated the escape to freedom for many. Maria Stewart also made significant contributions to the movement through her powerful speeches and other efforts.

The women's suffrage movement saw instances where black women experienced dual discrimination. Male leaders were reluctant to support them due to their race, while white feminists also failed to give them fair treatment because of their race. Nevertheless, Sojourner Truth, Ida B. Wells, and Mary Church Terrell all fought tirelessly for equal voting rights. Ida B. Wells worked extensively to investigate lynching activities targeting black individuals, while Mary Church Terrell actively participated in suffragette campaigns.

The Civil Rights Movement saw the vital contributions of Black women in the 1950s and 1960s, as they organized protests, led grassroots movements, and fought for racial equality. Icons like Rosa Parks, Ella Baker, Fannie Lou Hamer, and Dorothy Height were pivotal in driving change and confronting systemic racism.

The Black feminist movement arose to address the combined challenges of racism and sexism experienced by Black women. Figures such as Audre Lorde, Bell Hooks, Angela Davis, and Kimberlé Crenshaw emphasized the distinct struggles of Black women and promoted a comprehensive feminism that tackled issues of race, class, and gender.

Black women have achieved notable progress in the realm of political leadership, overcoming obstacles and laying the groundwork for future generations. Pioneers such as Shirley Chisholm, the first

Black woman elected to Congress, and Kamala Harris, the first Black

and South Asian woman Vice President of the United States, have

defied traditional limitations and motivated others to engage in

political activism.

 Black women have consistently shown resilience, bravery, and

perseverance in the course of history. Their activism has played a

crucial role in challenging oppressive systems and pushing for

societal transformation, making a lasting impact on the struggle for

equality and fairness. Sojourner Truth (1797–1883) was born into

slavery but became an advocate for abolition and women's rights.

Her well-known speech "Ain't I a Woman?" Challenged the

prevailing beliefs about gender and race. Truth was active in

advocating for abolition, women's suffrage, and social justice.

Ida B. Wells (1862–1931) was an investigative journalist who

brought to light the atrocities of lynching in the United States. She

was a co-founder of the National Association for the Advancement of

Colored People (NAACP) and the National Association of Colored

Women. Through her work, Wells raised awareness about racial violence and campaigned for civil rights and equality.

Mary Church Terrell (1863–1954) was both a suffragist and civil rights activist, known for co-founding the National Association of Colored Women. She dedicated her life to challenging racial segregation and discrimination and tirelessly advocated for educational and economic opportunities for Black women. Terrell was a leading advocate for both women's suffrage and racial justice.

Ella Baker, 1903-1986: She was a civil rights organizer and strategist who collaborated with the NAACP and the Southern Christian Leadership Conference, SCLC. A pioneer of the understanding of grassroots organizing and leadership of young people, Baker was part of the formation of the Student Nonviolent Coordinating Committee. The understanding of the power of collective action and the need for participants to govern themselves for change is highlighted by Baker, and her contributions have had a lasting impact on grassroots and participatory democracy.

Fannie Lou Hamer: a civil rights leader who, in conjunction with her organization of the Mississippi Freedom Democratic Party, established a series of voter registration drives and challenged racial segregation at great personal risk. Hamer's testimony at the 1964 Democratic National Convention was exceedingly powerful and exposed the struggle for the right to vote.

Shirley Chisholm, 1924–2005. The first Black woman elected to Congress, Congresswoman Chisholm represented New York's 12th congressional district. Along with then-Representatives Barbara Jordan of Texas and Gwen Moore of Wisconsin, she co-founded the Congressional Black Caucus and ran for the Democratic nomination for President in 1972, the first Black major-party candidate for president and for the first woman to run for the Democratic Party's presidential nomination.

These figures speak volumes of many Black women who have shaped political activism throughout history. Their courage, resilience, and greater dedication to social justice continue to inspire movements for change.

Long before Black women were engaging in politics, one could notice the women were black, female, and poor, which meant they were amid various forms of oppression. Notwithstanding, they have remained standing up and voice their rights and the communities. Here are some of their challenges:

Suffrage Movements—exclusion: While women were organizing to get suffrage, Black women were consistently left out from mainstream, white suffrage organizations. Racism within the suffrage movement also meant Black women could be pushed to the side or simply left out of the majority suffrage marches and events.

Systemic racism systematically denied Black women access to political participation. The use of Jim Crow laws and the fact that various voter suppression tactics like poll taxes and literacy tests made Black voters inaccessible, mainly in Southern states. This took away their ability to partake in the political process.

Sexism Within Black Communities: Black women were central to the broad struggle for civil rights, yet this was oftentimes cast in the shadow of sexism within their communities. Frequently, the male-dominated leadership structures circumvented and neglected the work of Black women as they were put at the fringes to support the leadership of men instead of them being seen as leaders in their own right.

Economic barriers: Many black women are at a disadvantage in ways that economic constraints can be used to limit their ability to participate in political activism. The economic disparities on matters of poverty, stemming from past injustices, such as slavery and segregation, meant more black women had to prioritize basic needs—such as food and housing—over activism or advocacy politics. Threats, Violence, and Intimidation: It was violence and intimidation that constituted the worst part of the resistance by black women who dared to challenge the status quo and fight for their rights. This ranged from physical violence by white supremacists to harassment and surveillance by law enforcement agencies.

Faced with all these challenges, Black women did not back down from political participation and founded grassroots movements and mobilized their communities to cause change. With resilient spirit and commitment, they paved the way for other activists, and their work contributed to civil rights and social justice movements in historic ways.

Chapter 2: The Civil Rights Movement and Beyond

The Civil Rights Movement owes a lot of black women. They played crucial roles in the Civil Rights Movement: playing the voices, exerting leadership, and providing labor in the struggle for equal opportunities for the races. Their roles were manifold and crucial to the success of the movement. This essay will critically analyze their roles.

Organization and Leadership: Black women were at the heart of organizing and leadership in grassroots movements. Leaders like Ella Baker, a proponent of participatory democracy and community organizing, have been instrumental in organizations like the Southern Christian Leadership Conference (SCLC) and the Student Nonviolent Coordinating Committee (SNCC). Their leadership often centered on empowering the local communities and marginalized voices.

Strategic Thinkers and Tacticians: Some of the Black women brought into the Civil Rights Movement strategic thinking and tactical innovation, including Septima Clark—dubbed the "Mother of the Movement" developed citizenship education programs empowering Black citizens to navigate the requirements for voter registration in the South. Fannie Lou Hamer led the Mississippi Freedom Democratic Party, challenging the segregationist policies of the Democratic Party.

Bridge Builders and Coalition Builders: Many of the black women who led the movement became bridge builders, finding ways to make coalitions between various groups in the struggle. They knew that solidarity was important and that it was best to fight from an intersectional standpoint. Dorothy Height became one of the primary bridge builders at the National Council of Negro Women; she worked to tie civil rights organizations together with women's-rights groups.

Community mobilizers and activists; Black women mobilized their communities, and participated in direct-action campaigns, boycotts, and protests among others. Among them include Rosa Parks, who refused to give up her bus seat and sparked the Montgomery Bus Boycott, and Diane Nash, who led the Nashville Student Movement, which addressed the potential power of nonviolent resistance and civil disobedience.

A few spokespersons have also been black women—but they have often been behind the scenes as caretakers and sustainers, providing the rest of the movement with logistical support such as food, shelter, and childcare. These women remained steadfast in their support and stayed there despite the violence and discrimination they faced.

Legal and Political Pioneers: In the legal and political arena, Black women also played significant roles during the Civil Rights Movement. Constance Baker Motley, who became the first Black woman to be appointed to the federal judiciary, and Barbara Jordan, who became the first Black woman to be elected to the Texas Senate since Reconstruction, both women were pioneers who brought change and opened doors for other Black women in legal and political careers.

The Civil Rights Movement has been characterized by a series of excellent contributions of Black women that challenged both systemic racism and sexism, exceeded the scope of political activism, and set the foundation for further struggles for social justice.

This is defined by legal scholar Kimberlé Crenshaw as an intersectionality concept, where one's identities intersect and combine to form systems of oppression and privilege. Thus, what is used when studying the intersection of race, gender, and class reveals a different kind of discrimination and disadvantage to arise from the interplay between these factors. Thus, race, gender, and class intersect:

Race and Gender- Women of color, for instance, experience both race and gender discrimination. They will, in turn, suffer from stereotypes and biases because of the combination of racism and sexism. Here are stereotypes such as the "angry Black woman" stereotype, which persists in perpetuating harmful stereotypes regarding Black women's emotions and behavior. As a result of the combination of racial and gender discrimination, black women would not be accorded opportunities in the workplace, education, healthcare, and so on.

Gender and Class- Women, especially women of color, are disproportionately located at the bottom of the income distribution, and have fallen further behind on this as workers' wages have stagnated. Gender bias intersects with economic inequality to create obstacles to economic security and upward mobility for women. Women from low-income families often confront barriers to high-quality child care, unequal wages, and inadequate healthcare. Such intersectional forms of oppression work to deepen the poverty of many women and heighten gender disparities in wealth and income.

Triple Oppression- Maltreated people are said to have "triple oppression" when belonging to a race-gender-class combination of oppression. For example, black women experience triple oppression of racism, sexism, and classism. Such triple oppression can be spotted in different fields of life from job and schooling to medical care and criminal contact.

What this says is that through understanding how different elements of race, gender, and class intersect, one can understand the complex systems of oppression and privilege. Pointing out the different types of discrimination and inequality that intersect can work to help create more inclusive, equitable systems that uplift and empower people from all communities. Rosa Parks, Ella Baker, and Fannie Lou Hamer were instrumental figures in the Civil Rights Movement, each making unique and significant contributions that shaped the course of history. Let's examine their contributions individually:

Rosa Parks, 1913–2005 is sometimes called the "Mother of the Civil Rights Movement" because of her crucial role in kick-starting the Montgomery Bus Boycott in 1955. On December 1, 1955, Parks refused to give up her seat to a white passenger on a bus that was still segregated in Montgomery, Alabama, which sparked a city-wide boycott that went on for more than a year. Parks' act of resistance mobilized the African American community and brought national attention to the issue of segregation and racial injustice in the United States. Her stance, full of courage, signified nonviolence as well as civil disobedience to fight for racial equality.

Ella Baker 1903–1986 was a grassroots organizer and activist who was instrumental in providing support to several civil rights organizations such as the Southern Christian Leadership Conference (SCLC) and the Student Nonviolent Coordinating Committee (SNCC).

She believed that grassroots organizing and ordinary people were the ones to create change and believed in ordinary people's strength. In 1957, she was part of the founding meeting of the Southern Christian Leadership Conference and later helped to establish the Student Nonviolent Coordinating Committee, which she helped charter in 1960. Through her leadership, Baker empowered both young activists and the voices of those who were marginalized in the movement. She believed in participatory democracy and the collective power of action.

Fannie Lou Hamer was a leader in the American civil rights movement and an activist in grassroots organizing and argumentative advocacy for voter rights. Born in Mississippi in 1917 and raised in a sharecropping family, she became involved in the Civil Rights Movement after she attended a voter registration workshop in 1962.

Undeterred by violence and intimidation, Hamer became a leader in the MFDP and led challenges to the Democratic Party's segregationist policies at the 1964 Democratic National Convention. Hamer's testimony before the Credentials Committee in the convention had brought attention from all over the nation to the civil rights movement's struggle for the right to vote.

As a whole, Rosa Parks, Ella Baker, and Fannie Lou Hamer all made indelible contributions to the Civil Rights Movement through their staging of these acts of leadership and commitment to just causes. This brave work inspired generations of activists and paved the way for significant advancements in civil rights and social justice in the United States.

Chapter 3: Black Feminism and Political Thought

Black feminist theory represents one of the frameworks examining the intersections of race, gender, sexuality, and class, focusing on the experiences and perspectives of Black women. It emerged from criticism against those limitations of mainstream feminist theory that tended to sideline the peculiar challenges faced by women of color and against mainstream civil rights discourse that often left matters of gender and sexuality aside. It aims to center the voices and experiences of Black women, to examine how multiple forms of oppression intersect and compound to form the lived realities of those who experience them.

Black feminist theory challenges the notion that the oppression that is experienced by gender is best understood in isolation from other systems of oppression. It recognizes that the Black woman experiences intersectional forms of discrimination and marginalization because of both race and gender, as well as class, sexuality, and other social identities. Black feminist theory also recognizes the diversity of experiences in the Black community, including issues of class, sexual orientation, disability, and immigrant status, all of which combine to shape the experience of race and gender and, thus, people's experiences of oppression and privilege.

The relevance of Black feminist theory to political equity lies in its ability to illuminate how systems of power operate to marginalize certain groups while privileging others. By centering the experiences of Black women and other marginalized groups, Black feminist theory provides a more comprehensive understanding of the complexities of oppression and the intersections of race, gender, and other social identities. This understanding is essential for developing inclusive and equitable political strategies and policies that address the needs and concerns of all members of society.

Furthermore, Black feminist theory highlights the importance of intersectional organizing and coalition-building in the fight for political equity. By recognizing the interconnectedness of various forms of oppression, activists can work together across different social movements to address the root causes of inequality and injustice. Black feminist theory emphasizes the importance of solidarity and collective action in challenging systems of power and building more just and equitable societies.

Black feminist theory reveals its relevance to political equity in the potential to shed light on how systems of power work to marginalize some groups while privileging others. Working from Black women and other marginalized groups' experiences, Black feminist theory has the potential for a more comprehensive view of the complexities of oppression, including the many social identities that may be involved. This kind of understanding is crucial when developing truly inclusive and equitable political strategies and policies that address the needs and concerns of all members of society.

Black feminist scholarship and activism were important in framing discourses on race, gender, and social justice. These encompass a very wide array of topics, including themes such as intersectionality, reproductive justice, identity politics, and grassroots movements. Important figures and their contributions include:

Audre Lorde was a poet, essayist, and queer activist whose work addressed the issues of race, gender, sexuality, and intersectionality of identity and oppression. In "Sister Outsider," a collection of essays, Lorde wrote about the intersections of identity and oppression to advocate for the empowerment of marginalized voices. Lord's work is a reminder of the power of self-love, self-care, and building community to be part of the drive toward freedom.

Bell Hooks was a cultural critic, feminist theorist, and writer who works examined the intersections of race, gender, and class. "Ain't I a Woman: Black Women and Feminism" challenged the mainstream feminist discourse over the exclusion of women of color from the feminist movement. Her works challenged the canons of power, identity, and liberation and identified the need for inclusion, intersectional feminism.

Patricia Hill Collins is a sociologist and author best known for her groundbreaking work in the area of intersectionality and Black feminist thought. She is best known for her book, "Black Feminist Thought: Knowledge, Consciousness, and the Politics of Empowerment," which is a seminal work in the field looking at the intersectionality of race, gender, and class in shaping the experiences of Black women. Thus, Collins's work has been influential in academic and activist circles, giving the framework for understanding the systems of oppression and resistance.

Kimberlé Crenshaw, a legal scholar and professor, is famous for introducing the concept of "intersectionality" and leading the development of critical race theory. She emphasizes how race, gender, and other social identities come together to produce distinct types of discrimination and inequality. Crenshaw's theory of intersectionality has been extensively embraced in feminist research and advocacy, influencing discussions on identity politics and societal fairness.

Barbara Smith is a writer, activist, and co-founder of the Combahee River Collective, a Black feminist organization. The Combahee River Collective Statement, which she co-authored with other members, expressed a Black feminist viewpoint that prioritized the experiences of Black women and called for the liberation of all marginalized individuals. Smith's activism has been dedicated to causes such as reproductive justice, LGBTQ+ rights, and anti-racist advocacy.

These individuals are just a small sample of the numerous Black feminist scholars and activists whose writings and activism have played a part in promoting social justice and empowering marginalized communities. Their work remains a source of inspiration and guidance for current movements seeking change.

Intersectionality, developed by Kimberlé Crenshaw, focuses on the interlocking aspects of social identity and the systems of oppression that stem from those identities. This means that people experience multiple forms of discrimination and privilege. Therefore, in the context of political organizing, intersectionality has deep implications for understanding power dynamics, building coalitions, and advocating for social change. Understanding Interlocking Systems of Oppression: The concept of intersectionality encourages organizers to understand that their experiences of oppression are not isolated from each other. Instead, they are shaped by the interlocking systems of power and privilege that exist in society. For example, a Black woman will be discriminated against based on her race and gender, thus creating varied cases of marginalization that cannot be appropriately pursued from a purely racial or gender perspective.

Focusing on Marginalized Voices: Intersectionality requires placing marginalized voices and experiences at the forefront of political organizing endeavors. This entails actively searching for and amplifying the viewpoints of individuals most impacted by systemic oppression. By prioritizing the voices of marginalized communities, organizers can create more comprehensive and successful approaches to addressing social inequality.

Encouraging Collaboration Among Movements: Intersectionality promotes the idea of organizers forming alliances across various social movements to tackle the interconnectedness of oppression. This means that movements for racial justice, gender equality, LGBTQ+ rights, environmental justice, and economic justice are linked, and working together can result in more holistic and effective solutions. Intersectional organizing acknowledges that problems like racism, sexism, homophobia, and economic inequality are deeply intertwined and should not be dealt with separately.

Acknowledging Privilege and Allyship- Intersectionality calls on individuals to acknowledge their privilege and position within power structures. It urges those with the privilege to support marginalized communities by using their resources, influence, and platforms to advocate for their fight for justice. Allyship based on intersectionality is based on humility, active listening, and a readiness to learn from those who are most impacted by oppression.

Championing Inclusive Policies and Practices- Intersectionality plays a crucial role in shaping inclusive policies and practices that cater to the varied needs and perspectives of marginalized groups. By taking into account the interconnected identities and experiences of people, advocates can strive for policies that advance fairness and equality for everyone. This could involve addressing matters like police violence, reproductive rights, health care accessibility, affordable housing, and immigrant rights, among other concerns.

The impact of intersectionality on political organizing is profound as it shapes organizers' understanding and approach to addressing systems of oppression, prioritizing marginalized voices, forming alliances across movements, acknowledging privilege and allyship, and promoting inclusive policies and practices. Embracing an intersectional approach allows organizers to strive for a fair and equitable society that supports and empowers individuals of all social identities.

Chapter 4: Contemporary Challenges and Struggles

Many of these challenges that women of color present in politics today are directly tied to a system that has perpetuated inequality. Although there is this progress, Black women still face existential hurdles of their own that stem from conditions allowing full participation and influencing power within political environments. In this regard, here are some key challenges:

Underrepresentation- Black women are grossly underrepresented in all elected offices at both state and federal levels. They make up a considerable portion of the electorate and are highly engaged in civic participation. Their representation in political leadership doesn't reflect their demographic presence.

Intersectional Discrimination: Black women suffer from intersectional discrimination from their race and gender. Stereotypes and biases based on racism and sexism subordinate their credibility, visibility, and electability as political candidates. This intersectional discrimination might manifest itself as negative media portrayals, voter suppression tactics, and barriers to fundraising and campaign support.

Structural Barriers- Political institutions and party systems present structural barriers to Black women's access to political power. Without access to financial resources, institutional support, and networks of influence, their ability to run for office and win elections, as well as advance their policy agendas, is greatly inhibited. Much too frequently, discriminatory practices such as gerrymandering and voter ID laws disproportionately disenfranchise the Black community, particularly Black women.

Oppressive Political Environment- Black women politicians are subjected to antagonism, harassment, and ostracism from their cohorts, constituents, and citizens. They experience misogyny—a confluence of sexism and racism targeted specifically at the Black female political leader, which undermines their power and authority as leaders. An inhospitable environment may discourage Black women from pursuing political careers or from seeking leadership roles.

Institutional support is another factor that impacts their political activities. More precisely, black women political candidates and elected officials in general have less institutional support from parties and organizations than white women. This refers to a weaker range of endorsements, reduced campaign resources, and generally fewer recruitment efforts directed at Black women candidates. The lack of institutional support is what eventually holds back Black women from effectively competing in electoral contests.

Policy Priorities Ignored- Marginalized or ignored throughout most mainstream political discourse are the policy priorities and concerns of Black women. Central to the lived experiences of Black women are such issues as reproductive justice, access to healthcare, criminal justice reform, economic inequality, and racial justice, which seldom give much heed by policy makers and leaders within the political realm. This requires a great deal of hard work to break down systemic barriers to representation, fight intersectional discrimination, and build truly inclusive political spaces.

Supporting political leadership and advocacy by Black women is vital for equity, justice, and democracy for all. Voter suppression, representation, and systemic barriers are interconnected issues that disproportionately affect marginalized communities, including Black women. Here's an analysis of each:

Voter suppression, representation, and systemic barriers are all interrelated issues that disproportionately affect communities of color, especially Black women. Here is a breakdown of each.

Voter Suppression: Voter suppression refers to the tactics and policies that restrict or impede eligible voters from exercising their right to vote. Such tactics disproportionately harm communities of color, young people, and low-income communities. Examples are strict voter ID laws, purging voter rolls, reducing polling locations in predominantly minority neighborhoods, gerrymandering, and disinformation campaigns.

Although there has been considerable progress, Black women remain disproportionately underrepresented in political leadership positions. Their absence from these positions denies them an opportunity to advocate for policies that advance racial and gender equity, systemic injustices, and community well-being. The need for more representation of Black women in politics must step ahead of systemic barriers, including voter suppression, institutional discrimination, lack of resources, and lack of pathways to leadership positions within political parties and institutions.

 Systemic Barriers- This includes the structural impediments and discrimination that limit access to political participation, representation, and power. These barriers disproportionately affect the political influence of marginalized communities. Systemic barriers include limited access to voter registration and polling locations in minority neighborhoods.

Gerrymandered electoral districts that dilute the voting power of communities of color Institutional discrimination in political parties and organizations that marginalize Black women candidates and leaders Insufficient resources and support for Black women political candidates in terms of fundraising, campaign infrastructure, and endorsements.

Hostile political environments marked by racism, sexism, and misogyny discourage Black women from entering the political sphere and becoming leaders. Addressive to broader efforts in voting rights, diversity and inclusion in political leadership, and systemic barriers.

This includes voter access policies, fighting voter suppression tactics, electoral reform like redistricting and ranked-choice voting, and investing in efforts to recruit, train, and advance Black women in politics. This helps get us closer to realizing a more equitable and representative democracy for all.

Chapter 5: Successes and Triumphs

Celebration of the achievements and milestones in Black women's political history serves the purpose of recognizing and keeping alive resilience, leadership, and contributions toward social progress. Here are some of the milestones and accomplishments:

Upon election into the United States Congress in 1968, Chisholm became the first Black woman elected into the United States Congress, sitting in New York's 12th congressional district. Chisholm was one of the pioneers for women and people of color in politics who brought to the forefront civil rights, women's rights, and social justice throughout her career.

Barbara Jordan Delivers Keynote Address in 1976 at Democratic National Convention: Barbara Jordan delivered the keynote address to the Democratic National Convention in 1976, making her the first Black woman to do so. What made her speech so great was that she made a splendid statement through her force in values: equality, justice, and democracy.

Back in 1992, Carol Moseley Braun became the first Black woman to be elected to the United States Senate, representing Illinois. Her election broke barriers and inspired many generations of Black women to seek political leadership.

The 2020 election of Kamala Harris as the Vice President of the United States: Kamala Harris was the first Black woman and first Asian American woman to be elected as Vice President of the United States in 2020. This first ran into the history of the United States in terms of the election marked a milestone of hope as it also broke barriers for women and people of color in leadership.

Stacey Abrams, the former state representative of Georgia, has been at the forefront of organizing voter mobilization efforts and fighting against voter suppression in Georgia. Abrams' grassroots organizing and advocacy played a pivotal role in the increase of voter turnout and flipping the state of Georgia blue in the 2020 presidential election and the 2021 Senate runoff elections

Multiple Black Women Serving in Congress:

Black women have been represented in the United States Congress for the past several years. There, a representative such as Representative Maxine Waters, Representative Ayanna Pressley, Representative Cori Bush, and Senator Kamala Harris before she was elected Vice President.

These achievements and milestones in Black women's political history represent milestones of more representation, equity, and inclusion in political leadership. They serve to remind us of the spirit of resilience, determination, and leadership of Black women in shaping the course of history and advancing social change.

A milestone in American political history, Kamala Harris's election was the first ever by a woman, the first Black person, and the first South Asian to be elected as a Vice President of the United States of America. Her victory inspired women and people of color all around the world.

Stacey Abrams' Voter Mobilization Efforts in Georgia. She led the charge against voter suppression and improved the turnout of Georgia voters through her organization, Fair Fight Action. Abrams's grassroots-style organizing helped flip Georgia blue in both the 2020 presidential elections and the 2021 Senate runoff elections, helping elect two Democratic senators.

When Cori Bush won the democratic primary of Missouri's 1st congressional district in 2020, she became the first black woman to be elected to the United States House of Representatives. Her election sets the stage for amplifying the voices of marginalized communities, building on grassroots activism.

Lucy McBath is a gun violence prevention advocate who lost her son to gun violence and ran for Congress in Georgia's 6th Congressional District in 2018. Her election to Congress has made her a leader on gun control measures as well as criminal justice reform.

Ayanna Pressley's Congressional Win: In 2018, Ayanna Pressley, a progressive activist and Boston city councilor, won a Democratic primary in Massachusetts's 7th congressional district. In doing so, she ousted a 10-term incumbent and became the first Black woman elected to Congress from Massachusetts.

Barbara Lee's opposition to the Authorization for Use of Military Force: Barbara Lee, a longtime congresswoman from California, was the only member of Congress to vote against the AUMF in 2001. Lee has been so staunchly opposed to the AUMF, which grants broad authority for the use of military force to confront the 9/11 attacks, that her vote has been hailed and cited as an example of taking a principled stand.

These examples highlight leadership, resilience, and impact within Black women in politics, showing ways they mobilized communities, advocated for change, and shaped policy at local, state, and national levels. Resilience and strength of Black women have always been a fact of the push to further advancement of social justice, civil rights, and equality across all times in history. Despite the intersecting forms of oppression and marginalization, Black women activists have consistently epitomized remarkable courage, determination, and leadership in the pursuit of justice and liberation. Some of these will be mentioned here:

Slave revolts, the Civil Rights Movement, and more, Black women have been at the forefront of the struggle, including opposing oppressive systems and bringing freedom and equality. Intersectional Activism: Black women's activism understands that race, gender, class, and other social identities are interconnected and thus advocates for justice by being intersectional. The activism of Black women speaks to the specific plight of the marginalized, offering waypoints toward dismantling intersecting forms of oppression

The most vocal black women activists often originate from and have deep roots within their communities. These leaders organize from the grassroots, support their communities, and uplift the marginalized. Bold Advocacy: Black women activists are not afraid to speak out against injustice, risking their safety, livelihoods, and reputations just to call out systemic racism, sexism, and other forms of discrimination.

Activist black women strategize with the use of a variety of tactics and strategies aimed at achieving their goals through direct action and civil disobedience, legal advocacy, and coalition building. Their strategic activism is situated within a dynamic framework of power and assessments of social change.

Black women have paved the way for future generations of activists and leaders, leaving a lasting legacy of resilience, strength, and empowerment. Their contribution to social justice movements continues to inspire and guide ongoing struggles to achieve liberation. Raising the voices, the experiences of black women activists, supporting their leadership, and giving honor to the contributions of Black Women to movements for justice and equity is what is quite necessary today, recognizing the resilience and strength of the Black Woman. This is not only for celebrating leadership but also for gaining focus in terms of reiterating that the experiences of Black Women must be centered as well as their leadership towards a more equitable and inclusive world for all.

Chapter 6: Looking Ahead

Looking toward the future, political activism by Black women has immense promise, not to say potentially, for social justice, equity, and systemic change. Some of the trends and possibilities emerging in the future include:

Continued Leadership and Representation: Black women will continue to have an increased seat at the table of leadership and representation at every level of government, from local government to the highest levels of national office. The increased presence of Black women in elected positions will continue to shape policy agendas, promote diversity in political leadership, and make the voices of all marginalized communities a part of the discussion.

The activism of Black women will continue to operate within the framework of intersectionality, where forms of oppression are seen as interconnected. Working toward holistic solutions to the root causes of systemic injustice, activists will center the experiences of Black women and other marginalized groups.

Black women's political activism will continue to pursue grassroots mobilization and organizing. Such will ensure that the power of the collective is mobilized to effect change at the local, state, and national levels. It is through building on the legacy of past movements that there will be continued direct action, voter mobilization, and advocacy campaigns through the moving forward of goals.

Black women activists will increasingly leverage technology and digital platforms to amplify their voices, rally supporters, and organize campaigns. Digital activism and online storytelling will play vital roles in shaping public discourse, raising awareness, and building solidarity across communities.

Black women activists will lead policy innovation and advocacy around the most pressing issues: the fight for racial justice, gender equity, economic inequality, access to quality health care, and environmental justice. Black women activists will center the experiences and needs of their communities through bold policy solutions.

Activism by black women is going to continue to foster global solidarity and collaboration, building in solidarity with activists and movements around the world. Through these connections between battles for justice, activists will work toward collective liberation and solidarity among different communities. A look into the future of Black women's political activism lies in intergenerational leadership, where older activists transfer knowledge, skills, and lessons learned from past struggles to emerging leaders.

What the future holds is that the political activism of Black women holds tremendous promise for driving transformational change and building a more just and equitable society. By entering the leadership, experiences, and priorities of Black women, activists will continue to challenge systems of oppression, build power from the ground up, and create a future where all people can thrive. We need some holistic strategies that will bring down systemic barriers, promote representation and participation, and advance justice and inclusion for everybody to reach greater political equity. These are key strategies:

Policy measures to ensure that voting rights are protected, including measures such as regulating voter suppression, such as through voter ID laws, and the much more dangerous practice of gerrymandering. Access to the ballot box: expansive provisions for automatic voter registration, early voting, same-day voter registration, and mail-in voting. Invest in voter education and outreach efforts—particularly those targeting historically disenfranchised communities.

Policy and practice efforts aiming at achieving more diverse representation in leadership positions within political office, whether party leadership or government appointments. Support recruitment, training, and advancement of candidates who are underrepresented and include women, people of color, LGBTQ+ individuals, and people with disabilities. Fosters inclusive political environments that value and support the diversity of perspectives, experiences, and leadership styles.

Engage in grassroots organizing and mobilization to empower marginalized groups, amplify their voices, and mobilize collective action for change. Resource, train, and support grassroots organizations and community leaders who work to address social, economic, and political issues from the grassroots level. Build coalitions and alliances of diverse communities and movements, finding solidarity, leveraging the collective power, and working toward shared goals.

Seek policy change to bring equity and justice to areas like criminal justice, health, education, housing, economic opportunity, and environmental justice. By putting the needs and priorities of marginalized communities at the center of policy design and the decision-making process, it will be ensured that policies will be responsive to the lived experiences of those most affected by systemic injustice. In addition, it will show strategic advocacy initiatives, like lobbying, litigation, public education campaigns, and direct action, which advance policy reforms and hold elected officials and other institutions accountable.

Encourage civic education and empowerment activities that provide empowered individuals with knowledge, skills, and resources enabling them to take an active part in the political process. This should involve investment in programs such as leadership development, mentorship, and civic engagement aimed at promoting more representation of the youth, women, people of color, and immigrants. Create a culture of civic participation and activism that extends to valuing and encouraging active contributions to the community and society. Thus, through these strategies, involving all sectors, stakeholders can achieve great steps in the direction of improved political equity, representation, and inclusion for every member of society.

As we look toward political equity and social justice continuing, let's issue a call of action for continued support and advocacy. Here's how all of us can contribute to this important effort:

Stay Informed: Learn about the issues of political equity, systemic injustice, and the experiences of marginalized communities. Keep up to date on current events, policy debates, and grassroots organizing efforts.

Use your privilege and platform to amplify the voices and experiences of the few who are generally marginalized—Black women, Indigenous peoples, people of color, LGBTQ+, immigrants, and people with disabilities—through platforms like social media and within your communities. Share their stories and make calls to action.

Advocate for the realization of political equity, representation, and inclusion at every tier, from the local to the national level. Call your elected officials, attend town hall meetings, and become involved in the advocacy efforts that help bring into law reforms and initiatives that further justice and equity for all.

Volunteer, and give donations in the form of money or any other useful resources, to grassroots organizations and community-led projects fighting for systemic injustices and empowering those at the margin. Participate in activities, share your skills and expertise, and coordinate the release of ideas.

Exercise your right to vote at the city, county, state, and federal levels. Encourage people around you to vote. Keep attending city council and school board meetings. Engage in other civic activities, such as becoming part of advocacy groups, organizing grassroots campaigns, and engaging.

Speak against injustice whenever you come across it—whether it is at your workplace, in your school, in your community, or in social circles. Challenge stereotypes and biases and discriminate against practices. Advocate for equal and inclusive policies and practices.

Build coalitions and solidarity across diverse communities and movements to create collective power and amplify the impact of the work. Understand the interrelated nature of struggles for justice and work towards common goals collaboratively.

During your engagement in advocacy and activism, take care of yourself and your well-being. Seek support from the community and loved ones, and recognize the importance of rest and resilience in sustaining long-term social change efforts.

In this sense, we can continue forward in a sort of solidarity with marginalized communities toward advancing the cause of political equity, justice, and liberation for all by taking collective action. Together, we can create a society that becomes inclusive, equitable, and just for the present and future generations.

Conclusion

By centering Black women within political discourse, we move beyond equity into issues of inclusion, justice, and democracy. I end with these final musings on why centering the voices and experiences of Black women is so crucial:

Black women experience multiple forms of oppression that intersect along the dimensions of race, gender, class, and beyond. Centering Black women within political discourse allows us to see how systems of oppression work, and how individual people are impacted. Black women have been leaders of social justice movements and politically powerful people as far back as the 19th century. They are underrepresented in political institutions and decision-making forums. Focusing on Black women in political discourse ensures their voices are heard and their perspectives are included in policy-making and governance.

The policy priorities of Black women differ from those of other groups by the experiences and challenges they endure. Centering Black women in political discourse means policies that are central to their lives—racial justice, reproductive rights, health care access, economic inequality, and reforms in criminal justice—will be made. Black women are natural coalition builders; they bring people together across racial, gender, and class lines to advance a set of shared goals and interests. By centering Black women within political discourse, we build coalitions across these lines, strengthening movements for social change and liberation across all communities. The centering of Black women within political discourse holds political leaders and institutions accountable for addressing the needs and concerns of the marginalized. They ensure policies and practices promote equity, justice, and human rights for all members of society.

In conclusion, centering Black women in political discourse is not only a matter of representation but fundamentally a way of building an inclusive and equitable democracy. The listening, valuing, and amplification of the voices and experiences of Black women will allow us to create a political landscape expressing the diversity, resilience, and aspiration of every person.

www.ingramcontent.com/pod-product-compliance
Lightning Source LLC
Chambersburg PA
CBHW061312250726
48653CB00002B/913